The Barking Book

CRISTIANE F. S. PEDOTE

The Barking Book

EDITORA
Labrador

Copyright © 2020 by Cristiane F. S. Pedote
All rights reserved to Editora Labrador.

Editorial coordination
Pamela Oliveira

Copydesk
Marcia Men

Graphic design, formatting and cover
Felipe Rosa

Proofreading
Renata de Mello do Vale

Editorial assistance
Gabriela Castro

Cover image
Flavia Schwartzman

Cataloging-in-Publication Data (CIP)
Angélica Ilacqua – CRB-8/7057

Pedote, Cristiane F. S.
 The Barking Book / Cristiane F. S. Pedote. – São Paulo : Labrador, 2020.
 64 p.

ISBN 978-65-5625-069-4

1. Brazilian poetry I. Title

20-3195 CDD B869.1

Index for Systematic Catalog:
1. Brazilian poetry

EDITORA
Labrador

Editora Labrador
Editorial director: Daniel Pinsky
Rua Dr. José Elias, 520 — Alto da Lapa
São Paulo/SP — 05083-030
Phone number: +55 (11) 3641-7446
contato@editoralabrador.com.br
www.editoralabrador.com.br
facebook.com/editoralabrador
instagram.com/editoralabrador

The reproduction of any part of this work is illegal and constitutes an undue appropriation of the intellectual and patrimonial rights of the author.

The publisher is not responsible for the content of this book.
The author is responsible for the facts and judgments contained herein.

For Max

FOREWORD

What a privilege it has been to accompany Cristiane on her journey of self-inquiry and personal growth by reading *The Barking Book!*

The poems are an account of her experience entering in a love relationship. They are an open window to her soul. We ride the waves of her emotions: fear, confusion, rage, and glory. We feel her trepidation and her joy. And, we are happy for her when she comes out of the experience as a grander and richer person.

It takes great courage to write a book like this because in it, Cristiane exposes herself so publicly.

It takes great courage to search the depths of your soul for understanding and answers. But, if you knew Cristiane as long as I do, it would come as no surprise.

The English word 'courage' comes from the French words 'coeur' (heart) and 'rage' (rage) and that is exactly why Cristiane wrote these poems. Her heart was in a rage! She had to do it! The words were barking out of her – forcing their way out. And, how lucky we are to be at the receiving end of it!

I have been fortunate to watch Cristiane boldly explore the world since our paths crossed seven years ago, when I had the distinct pleasure of working for her at a global Wall Street firm. While she was a gifted strategist, what I remember most about her then was having the courage to put people first and to drive cultural change against a rigid system. When she left Wall Street to start her own social impact enterprise, Pulsara, it came as no surprise to me because I had already seen her listen to her soul and feed it as needed. With Pulsara, she transforms lives materially and spiritually, connecting people and businesses so they rise to their full potential. Through Pulsara, she gets to put into action all the wisdom she has accumulated through years of self-reflection, from trying oh-so-many things and from the courage of living through transformations consciously.

Here and now, we all get to witness another daring chapter in her life: writing this, her first book. As she continues to explore her creative side, I cannot help but envision a rose slowly opening, revealing beautiful layer after beautiful layer, releasing its sweet scent to the world.

Toni Cortese

ACKNOWLEDGEMENTS

I want to thank Flavia Schwartzman for her friendship, companionship and for the photo that illustrates the cover of this book; Lucas Tauil de Freitas, Luciana Vichino, and Toni Cortese for taking the time to read the manuscript and encouraging me to publish it; Juliana Porto Montellano for bringing the depths of myself to light; and Lama Tsering Everest for being the light on my path.

I bark at you
you bark back at me
I bite, you like
until you don't like it anymore
Or is it that barking and biting became just too sad?
You stay
I go
Ok?
Ok.

Paraty, 09 de janeiro de 2020

Blue
Here I am
Crossing
Come meet me

Paraty, 11 de janeiro de 2020

It was there
Hidden in plain sight
Horns that fly
Lakes that burn
Tresses defying gravity
Weaved by healing hands
Both present and absent

São Paulo, 12 de janeiro de 2020

Can you see?
What?
The waves.
Maybe.
Maybe what?
If I squint my eyes.
You don't have to.
I know, but I want to.
Do you?
Maybe.
Maybe what?
If you hug me.
What?
It's a song.
Let's dance then.
Ok, but first.
What?
Can you see?

São Paulo, 13 de janeiro de 2020

There you are.
What took you so long?
I got lost.
Did you?

You didn't?
Yes, a little, but then it started to rain and I stopped.
You shouldn't have.
I know, but it was beautiful
Those tears
They are for her
A gift.
She would have enjoyed.
Would she?
Yes.

São Paulo, 14 de janeiro de 2020

Does it hurt?
Blue, answer me.
Blue.
He can't.
Why not?
Why don't you come join us?
I'm afraid.
That is wise of you.
Blue, Blue, Blue.
Repeating his name will not do it.
What will then?
The right question.
Is there such a thing?

São Paulo, 15 de janeiro de 2020

There I was
Daring to be old
Confident
Ripe
Blue

São Paulo, 16 de janeiro de 2020

Eyes that breathe
Air, I need more of it.
It's coming.
How?
It's coming.
Air
Breathe, breathe.
It's not coming...
I am here.
Yes, but I will go alone.

São Paulo, 17 de janeiro de 2020

You played
I danced
The sand dunes
The sea beyond
I know now
To which tale this scene belongs
Do you?

São Paulo, 18 de janeiro de 2020

She is there.
I know.
Did she have to?
She chose to.
Would you?
I have to.

São Paulo, 19 de janeiro de 2020

Blue
The joy
Unexpected
Beautiful
I am afraid to say more
Why?
Is it really you?
What does your heart say?
It says yes.

São Paulo, 20 de janeiro de 2020

From up there
I kept swimming
Clouds, leaves, bugs
Left it all behind
Kept going
Bigger, bigger
Then I saw him
and we bowed to each other
Happy
Thrilled
Buzzing

São Paulo, 21 de janeiro de 2020

Fear
Laughter covered the
bitter sound of the splashing frustration
It was all there
Void
It resurfaced the next morning in loud hope, which
soon drowned leaving the cookies untouched

São Paulo, 22 de janeiro de 2020

Caged.
Open it.
I am caged.
Open it.
Gone
Give me your hand.
Why now?
Why not?

São Paulo, 23 de janeiro de 2020

Where did you go?
What were you thinking?
I wasn't, I felt it.
Patience was in order.
I thought so.
Now what?
I run.

São Paulo, 24 de janeiro de 2020

An intense melting urge takes full hold
Exquisite
Divine
In a trance we dance
Holding it until we can hold it no more
and yet
We do

São Paulo, 25 de janeiro de 2020

Blue
Glowing in the unfathomable sea
Answering my call
Where to now?
Does it matter?
Keep it shining, then.
I will.

São Paulo, 26 de janeiro de 2020

The burning
Whirling and whirling and whirling
Again, again!
Clinging
Blue

São Paulo, 27 de janeiro de 2020

Where does it begin?
Isn't it when?
No, no, no... It's fading.
So, go play it again.
Will it suffice?
You won't know unless you try.

São Paulo, 28 de janeiro de 2020

Truth
So I tried and it grew, igniting the silence
The language you speak
And I am learning to decipher
To sing in tune
Blue

São Paulo, 29 de janeiro de 2020

Strong
Holding still a heart aching in despair
Harsh, brazen
Bursting naked
Alive

São Paulo, 30 de janeiro de 2020

Come
We are waiting
Fret not, dear one
We are waiting
In the silky darkness
We are waiting
Come as you are
We are waiting

São Paulo, 01 de fevereiro de 2020

Depths layered with lightness
Written over the centuries
Coming free
Powerful and purposeful
Beautiful
Blue

São Paulo, 3 de fevereiro de 2020

You came
I changed
It felt old
Undeserving
So I plunged in the gap you sustain unknowingly
And resurfaced
Erect
Glorious

São Paulo, 4 de fevereiro de 2020

Wanting became tired and opened
To Touch
May I?
Thrill rose
Eager
In joyful surrender

São Paulo, 5 de fevereiro de 2020

Maddening voices
Lost and confused
Angry
Ah, the anger
Erupting in overpowering rage
Never-ending
Never

São Paulo, 6 de fevereiro de 2020

Fuming in rage
We fought into the night
Then I remembered her words and awoke to lemons
   and sheets of flowers washing over the rumba

São Paulo, 11 de fevereiro de 2020

Choked
The silent screaming rage exposes the fangs full of
   dripping venom that blinds the heart and darkens
   the sky of the soul that lies scorched
Lost

São Paulo, 14 de fevereiro de 2020

The ride was bumpy
It left me wiser
I hear you.
I hear you.
Good.
I mean it.
I know.
Good? What about Bad?

São Paulo, 15 de fevereiro de 2020

Ugly, grotesque, brute
Disguised as beauty
So collected
So centered
Come! Come!
Come naked!
Disheveled
Wild
Free

São Paulo, 17 de fevereiro de 2020

What to say?
When I find myself here again,
Caught
In invisible chains
Dragging and dreading to plunge?
I breathe
Suspending the grasp
The jaw opens and the biting stops
For now

Khadro Ling, 21 de fevereiro de 2020

Crawling back
Up and down and down some more
Long horns calling
Blue rose grey golden
Spraying timidly
I see you
Deep there
Rolling

Khadro Ling, 23 de fevereiro de 2020

Suspended
In and out
Words
Blowing cold what was golden before
Greetings whispered through the mist
Once the door was closed

Khadro Ling, 26 de fevereiro de 2020

Life
A never-ending vortex
The shadow of what will become
Sparkling with dew drops while the fire mounts and
    the offerings are made

Khadro Ling, 28 de fevereiro de 2020

Beauty
Blasting open the fabric tightly woven
The tongue came first
Shivering
Then it was time to go

São Paulo, 02 de março de 2020

Care
To give freely
Going beyond yourself
For us

São Paulo, 05 de março de 2020

Urge
Greeted by sigh
Moved at a different pace
Made room for pause and the wish
For more

São Paulo, 08 de março de 2020

Freedom
It comes at a cost
I am willing Blue, I truly am.
Today maybe. What about tomorrow?
Does it matter?

São Paulo, 26 de março de 2020

So I crossed

The mask was so tight I forgot
Thought it was for real
There was beauty though
Yes, that I will treasure

São Paulo, 28 de março de 2020

I have landed
The giant is there
In the tower I wait
Gray shadows luminescent sound quiet when I close my eyes
Come, reveal yourself
We have already met
Now, as before

São Paulo, 08 de abril de 2020

Our paths are crossing
South west of the border
Where time took a turn
Then stopped
For us

São Paulo, 08 de abril de 2020

You shine
In the depths of me you grew strong until it was time
   to part
To brighten
Our lives
You shine
For 29 years and a thousand more
You shine

São Paulo, 22 de abril de 2020

Mother

Blessed are those who shelter under your wings

Glorious woman warrior

Healer of body and soul

To you I bow my head touching the ground

Mother

São Paulo, 23 de abril de 2020

A sigh leaves me
Silent music playing inside and out
Wait.
Wait.
Now.

São Paulo, 02 de maio de 2020

You came
And stayed just long enough, as to make sure I saw you
You came
Knowing I had heard your call and was getting ready to fly
You came
Soon we will be crossing the skies
And together we will land

São Paulo, 10 de maio de 2020

Swimming
Down below where the roots are deep there is room
Room for what?
For me and you.
And for us?
Us? We don't take any space.

São Paulo, 30 de maio de 2020

This book was composed by Janson Text LT Std 11 pt and
printed in Pólen 90 g/m² by graphic Paym.